Purple Petals

Bruised Flowers

A Mentor's Journey

by Wanda J. Evans

To order additional copies of this book, contact:
Xlibris
1-888-795-4274
www.Xlibris.com
Orders@Xlibris.com

Book Designer: Alfred B. Ilagan

ISBN: 978-1-4257-2481-8 (sc)
ISBN: 978-1-4257-2895-3 (hc)
ISBN: 978-1-4771-6347-4 (e)

Library of Congress Control Number: 2006907031

Print information available on the last page

Rev. date: 07/09/2020

Dedication

To my three children, Langston, Stevie , and Sydney. In spite of all of the kids I have brought home, moved in, and mentored, you have never complained, competed, or expressed jealousy. I cannot imagine how you view me as a parent; however, every time I look at each one of you, I know that I did something right. On the days that I wanted to quit, your smiles, jokes, and laughter have helped to remind me why I do the work that I do. Although I have loved many other children, none can replace the love I feel for each one of you. I gave you life, but the three of you have given me a reason to continue to live.

<u>Special Thanks</u>

To my husband Steven, who worked vigorously to help me set up my manuscript. I really appreciate all the nights that you lay in bed listening to me share my vision. I could not have gotten my book completed without your assistance and support. You have truly been my best friend in this process.

Thank you, Nick Mathis, for your original drawing. I loved the girl with a broad nose and full lips from the time that I laid eyes on her. I pray that you allow your many talents to take you beyond the "concrete jungles" of Chicago. Your generosity will remain in my spirit forever.

Foreword

The color purple occupies an interesting space in the color spectrum. The color has passion; it invokes feelings of substance and universal harmony. The passion can be felt in the primal notes from the song, "Purple Haze" by the late Jimmy Hendrix. The syncopation, driving guitar rhythms, and soulful vocals heighten the inner spirit and feed the soul.

In the best selling novel, *The Color Purple*, by Alice Walker, the color purple again captures human universality. It illuminates the ubiquitous struggle between good and evil, passion and pain. The novel departed on a journey of pathos and arrived at a destination of triumph.

The organization Purple Rain: Girls Overcoming Abuse, started and headed by Wanda Evans, is an anomaly in its time. The focus of the group is to help female teenagers who are battered and abused by their significant others. The group is about truth in a world where today's icon is tomorrow's inconsequential.

Wanda Evans, through Purple Rain, has cast aside the primal selfish forces that hold most of us in bondage. Her clarity of mission and purpose and personal knowledge of self has prepared her for her journey. It is evident that she knows herself. She reaches out and empowers herself in a complex way. This knowledge enables her to reach out and empowers her to say not only can I help but also I *will* help. Her efforts help us to live in a world that we don't understand but must accept and to express love even while we expose our own human vulnerability.

James Russell

Preface

In my own adult life, abuse came full circle. I like to say that when I wasn't looking, I fell in love with a man who became my abuser. On a good day, he was fun, funny, and passionate; on a bad day, he was a walking ball of jealousy and rage, and I was the canvas upon which he painted his red, blue, and purple pain. I was his walking work of distorted art and by the end, an emotional wreck. I dated him for two years before I got strong enough to do a complete autopsy on the relationship. Through the autopsy, I discovered that he was sick, but I was sicker because I was actively participating in letting someone dehumanize me in the name of love. Even with the autopsy complete, it still took me another year before I completely ended the relationship. When I say ended it, I mean ended it. I cut ties with all joint friends, including his mother who had been very kind to me and his aunt whom I'd met while an undergrad. I moved to the other side of town. I stopped returning phone calls. In fact, we only spoke if he called and I just happened to switch over from the other line.

The most important step that I took was to stop having intercourse with him. This may seem small, but for our relationship, it was huge. In spite of the abuse, we'd always had a dynamic sex life. This one area hadn't been tainted. Often times, it was the one area that gave me hope. I thought that our passion could fix things. He was tender, calm, and reflective in bed. We dreamed together there; we shared secrets and goofy teen blunders. I more than liked the man that lay next to me and spoke of childhood hurts. I loved him. As silly as it may sound, it was real for me, and I didn't want to lose it. I didn't want to lose the part of him that was trapped in this vicious cycle of outbursts and torment. I kept trying to figure out how to separate the beauty from the beast but to no avail.

It wasn't long before I realized that in order to keep him, I would have to have a modern day lobotomy or become a "Stepford Wife." I'd have to lose all semblance of myself, particularly if it threatened him. I believe in "fair exchange no cheating." In the end, I couldn't do it, and I fought to dismantle the relationship. That was a long time ago, and although I've thought about those periods in my life from time to time, I spent far more time compartmentalizing those experiences until I started teaching in a high school on the Westside of Chicago. It was there that I started seeing girls get slapped, punched, and choke-walked in the hallways. It was there that I watched beautiful young women, some who even had children, come to school with black eyes and bite marks. It was there that I watched brilliant girls lose focus and interest in learning. It was there that I learned why God had allowed domestic violence to be listed in the index of my life story. He had a plan for me. It was already written. Thus, I'm no longer surprised that with the help of some pretty heroic students, I developed **Purple Rain: Girls Overcoming Abuse.**

This book of prose and poetry is about more than a teacher discovering the existence of intimate partner abuse in the high school setting. Quite honestly, the problem was always there. I just had not allowed myself to connect with it, or should I say, re-connect with it in order to feel driven enough to do anything about the issue. This book is not even completely about developing a support group for teen girls, although that effort was the catalyst for many interesting things. It is really a mentor's journey—a direct look at the growth and healing that can occur when everyday people step forward and share their own insecurities, frailties, and pain. It is about what can happen when people decide to care even if it seems like an uphill struggle. It is about big dreams coming true on shoestring budgets. It is about finding something to fight for and sometimes someone if need be. It is about the girl inside the woman and the woman becoming. It is about me. It is about you. In short, it is about all the purple petals and bruised flowers I have nurtured on my road to enlightenment and self-love.

Mission Statement

Purple Rain (PR) is a woman-based not-for-profit organization that provides support to teen girls who are currently or have been involved in abusive relationships. PR is dedicated to supplying support through a twelve-month integrated curriculum by providing a safe haven where girls from all walks of life can gather, share, and realize their options as they apply to relationships and their own lives. Our mission is to teach the girls to speak in truth while taking a close look at their choices. Counseling and a self-help guild are the core foundation for helping, while blending the arts with a girl's own life lessons will be used as a catalyst to seek emotional healing and develop positive self-worth while connecting with God. PR is committed to post-care in order to break the cycle of abuse by offering the girls who successfully complete the program job readiness, improved life management skills, and college planning.

You Broke Me

You broke me
Like the sticks
That are used
By the Scouts
Continual rubbing
Of nerves
Building friction
Inside walls
Causing smoke
To seep up
Creating an unwanted current
In a perfect wind
Or rather breeze
That kept our love at ease
While I aimed to please
You
Broke
Me

Down
And I struggle to get up
While my heart
Wants to combust
Instead, I implode
Exhausted by the load
You dumped inside my vessel
Unable to wrestle myself free
I no longer know me
Stay frightened by we
Or should I say us
Un-earthed secrets
Lead to disgust
And emotional disconnect
Not able to plug in
Don't know where to begin
To explain
The shame
Simply
Broke *me*

Where Do I Start

I don't know where to start. How do I begin to explain the evolution of Purple Rain? I wish that I could say something cool like all my life I've wanted to work with girls or that I spent so many years outraged at the abuse of women at the hands of men that I just had to act, but I can't. I was kind of just going along, a woman among girls, not really allowing myself to connect with them on an emotional level. I've always been much more comfortable among men. This has not been for any sexual reasons, I just simply related to their right to have a drive, to break rules, to be full-fledged leaders. I liked the fact that men are not told to "be nice." In fact, their aggression is celebrated. You can walk into any sports bar in America and see direct proof of that. They are not expected to apologize for having a vision and exuding confidence. On the contrary, they are encouraged to self-analyze, size up the opponent, knock it down, and push further.

Girls never quite receive that message except by happenstance and even then, she usually has to have a rich daddy to back her. The average girl is expected to look good, give good sex, and find a mate. If he is bald headed, blind, or ugly, "It don't matter if he got cheddar." They say that "a mind is a terrible thing to waste," yet girls often do. More often than not, they waste it for love. Girls give up all kinds of hobbies and interests in a direct effort to oblige someone that they are dating and in the worst cases, they actually give up themselves.

On the other hand, boys are constantly reminded not to let a girl get in the way of their opportunities. They are told from day one, girls are a dime a dozen, another one will come along, and she'll probably even be prettier. It's no wonder that I've struggled to identify with being a girl. It's hard to feel valued even when you're smart and talented.

In fact, those two qualities get girls in more trouble than one could imagine. They have to fight for the right to be received as bright and talented wherever they go, even when they order food. I didn't know it at the time but eventually I would have to face that truth while looking in the beautiful yet bruised faces of my female students. Of course, I had no idea that their scars and personal stories of pain would lead me back to once-charted territory and beyond. If I knew, I might not have been up for the challenge. It's hard to care about people. It's even harder to get them to care about themselves.

At different points in my life, I've been politically and socially active. However, as conscious as I have been about world issues, I never thought about intimate issues such as domestic violence. I can't really even explain why. It just wasn't something that I thought about even though I grew up in a house of domestic violence. For years, we were that house on the block that the police occasionally visited. I still remember, rather vividly, the police encouraging my father to leave and come back later, once he had cooled off. There is no way that I could ever forget the skillful way that my mother always fought back. She was the queen of good fighting tactics. Without a doubt, I can say that she fought to win. Her choice of weapons demonstrated that point. They varied from kitchen knives to hammers to plain "ole" hot chicken grease.

To my horror, she never hesitated to use any of them in the heat of rage or rather passion. It wasn't uncommon after all that fighting to hear my parents having sex, which meant that all that stuff she told us about leaving and not taking it anymore was officially null and void. We were not going anywhere.

<u>Wish I Had Not Been Silent</u>

I wish I had not been silent when they fought.
Shameful, ignorant people
Even at her funeral, it was
all about them needing
space to make a point
Fingers looking like
The tips of daggers
Ready to cut in the direction
Of the target
I sat
Mouth closed
Anxiety thick
Like the dark clouds
That gather before
An impending storm
You sat
You were
Defiantly comfortable
Showing who the boss is
Not really dealing with
The fact that the "real" boss
Of us all
Had sent his Angel of Death
Leaving tears
Delivering dim kisses
Breathless hugs
Empty smiles
Hollow hearts
Full of uncontrolled
Pounding and pounding
With enough air to penetrate
The hatred laced exchanges of
Two grown kids
Determined to do a "Trilla in Manilla"
On the very day, we were forced to kiss
An 8-year-old embalmed body
With wax hair and make-up farewell
While everyone was commenting
"They did a great job"
They forgot to mention that
You didn't
I should not have been silent, but
I didn't know how to scream

Why They Come

Young people become interested in your group for many different reasons, most of which have nothing to do with your mission or vision. Some decide that they really like hanging with their friends and they express interest in staying close to them. Other young people pursue your group as a pastime. They like one or two of your activities; however, they have no intention of getting better or becoming more involved. Some young people live in such horrid circumstances that they just aren't ready to go home and they see your group as a safe haven. Some just admire you. Therefore, it's a way to "kick-it" with their favorite person. Their reasons, though very different in nature, each bring their own set of problems—particularly when you never viewed them as someone that you wanted to mentor or even worse when you don't even like that particular youth very much.

Now please don't be shocked by the phrase, "didn't like that particular youth." Just like there are adults that you don't like, there are children that rub you the wrong way. I used to always say most times if you follow the kid home, you'll find out why. Other times, you may not like a young person because they remind you of someone who hurt or traumatized you in your youth. You are revisiting feelings of sadness and anger that you're not yet ready to work through. The reasons are varied, but they are real.

Imagine the young person who is excessively demanding or functions as a "small time bully." It is hard to feel fondly towards youth that pick on other youth for sport or forget that you're an adult, and they get in your face to assert power. What about when they are too "baby like." I have had 18-year-old males and females who were still sucking their thumbs and who had children of their own. One boy, when asked to work on not doing that publicly, quickly told me, "It doesn't bother my chics." In other words, he didn't see anything wrong with it. It was embarrassing to the other members in the group, not to mention the sanitary issue. I have had mentees whose every other word was an expletive no matter how much I worked with them. There are those that constantly lie. In fact, they lie so often, they often forget what they have shared. Even when they are telling the truth, a third of that is usually a lie.

Occasionally, I have encountered young people that steal. They don't always just blatantly steal; many just borrow and never return items. When you ask for it back, they play confused. Some will even ask you to loan them a couple of dollars to get something to eat or for bus fare and you'll learn later that they actually had a pocket full of money, but they didn't want to spend theirs. It is intensely hurtful to discover that a young person has used and manipulated you. Experience it and see how much you like that kid afterwards. Without a doubt, young people can give you a lot of reasons not to enjoy their company.

I have met young people upon first sight; I could tell that my school year was going to be rough. Hurt youth harbor a lot of hate and sometimes rage toward people and things that have made them feel powerless. Most of them have never learned how to manage or process pain. If you are lucky, they won't see you as someone towards which to direct it. However if you're unlucky, and many teachers are, they will often use you as a target.

Therefore, yes, it is possible not to like certain young people and sometimes, even when you are nice, young people don't like you either. That doesn't mean that you can't work with them. It does mean that you have to be conscious of yourself when you are interacting with them. It is one of the most important steps to becoming a great mentor. You must keep a pulse on your mind-set because harboring ill feelings towards a young person sets up an unpleasant struggle inside any mentoring group, and there is virtually no way to hide it. Young people notice everything, and true feeling have a way of leaking through sharp glances, indifferent laughs, and half-hearted hugs. It has always been my policy to be honest with young people, especially when they ask me. I have had youth ask me, "Why don't you like me?" and I'll tell them that I don't enjoy their company because they are dishonest or because they use excessive foul language or brutalize other youth. Unbelievably, most kids would cut a deal with me. They usually ask me, "If I stop doing that, then will we be cool?" In general, I reply, yes. Even if in my heart, I believe that they will never change. Mentors have to give youth second chances. There is always the possibility that they have learned to want something different for themselves. We have to have faith in the human spirit in spite of all its complexities. More often than not, if a young person has any level of respect for you, or if they think you have involved them in something special, they will try to eliminate the problem. You must stay open to meeting them halfway.

One would assume that every time you mentor a young person that you are fond of things would run smooth and that you would see tremendous growth. I'm here to tell you that more often than not, the young person that you love the most, the one in which you see the greatest potential, the one that you have let deep in your inner circle and close to your emotional core, is the very one that will not only disappoint you but will also break your heart. My best lessons in mentoring usually come from young people who I initially dislike. They are usually the ones that force me to really take a deep look at myself. What I say I am all "about." Why I say I am involved with mentoring. How I handled awkward situations.

Mentors have to accept that whether they like them or not, they are coming. In the end, why they come is unimportant. How we respond to them when they arrive is paramount. Our interaction will answer all pending questions more often than not; we learn that we needed to teach one another something.

Porcelain Doll

She is a porcelain doll
Beautiful and fragile
More for display
Than active play
After all, everyone knows
That you don't take porcelain
To the park
But he did
Despite advice
To simply protect and maintain
He chose to
Stuffed her in his book bag
Run real fast down bumpy streets
He chose to
Place her on the giant slide
And push her down head first
He chose to
Sit her on a baseball diamond
And hit baseballs her way

Today
It's hard to tell
What she is
Porcelain is so frail
And easily cracked
With shotty patchwork
He tried to fix her back
To the way, that he found her
He even surrounds her
With other pretty porcelain things
That washes out her appeal
It is unreal, the work he put into
Destroying her worth
She sits alone now
On a back shelf
He concluded that she's not
Good enough for display
Most don't even look her way
Fractures, splits, and cracks
Draw little attention
He doesn't have the heart to even mention
That he is responsible for the breaks
That sealed her porcelain fate
That damaged her delicate form
That left her torn.

When I First Started Mentoring

When I first started mentoring in the area of domestic violence, I didn't really know what I was doing. All I really knew was that within one year, over nine different girls approached me about an abusive situation happening in their life. All but one was a direct result of dating. I had one girl who was an incest survivor. Her mother had actually sided with the abuser, who of course was the mom's boyfriend. It was affecting every aspect of her teen life choices, particularly dating. I also knew that I believed women to be the laughter, music, and sunshine of the world and that they weren't meant to be punching bags. The thought of being young, and in high school, and getting beat up was just too much to fathom. I really kind of figured that the reason it's called domestic violence is because you and the person live together in a domestic situation. I had no idea that young teen males were becoming obsessive and controlling while still living at home with their own families. I didn't realize that young women in large numbers were accepting that behavior as normal.

I had a lot to learn and eventually a lot to do because whether I was ready or not, the girls kept coming. Once they learned that I had reached out to one, they brought others. What do you do when a young person is standing there with fear in their face or a black eye and they ask, "Do you have a minute to talk?" You find a minute to talk. They came before school, after school, before class, after class, they approached me in the hallways and even in the rest room. They continued to come until I responded.

I tried the quick talks. I tried long talks. I tried leading them to the social worker of the school; they weren't the least bit interested in that. They had decided that they felt safe with me. I even tried just giving them literature on the topic and trusting that they would read it. As you can imagine, that did not work very well. The last thing that you want to do when someone is causing you physical harm is read. It does not matter if it holds some truth or not. I knew it would not work, but I just did not feel like sticking my hand in quicksand to pull out a heart.

Truthfully, I could not even understand what I had done that caused all these young women to come forward and express such intensely deep pain to me. It wasn't like I ran a girl's groups or coached any girl's teams. It was as if I sat a neon sign outside my classroom, which read "dumping ground for the hurt." I actually tried to somewhat ignore or at least contain how deeply involved I was going to get into their personal situations. By no means did I really want to revisit that kind of sadness and sorrow. I had been through my own fire. Mine was a long time ago when I was young and inexperienced, but it happened. Why go digging up the past. I survived my own Tsunami. Who in his or her right mind would sign up for someone else's? The girls gave me the answer to that question. ME.

Mentors need to be aware that youth are always watching them, and they can tell which mentors genuinely care. They have incredible radar to pick up love signals. In fact, it seems to me that the more depleted they are in that area, the sharper they are in identifying love. At-risk youth don't always know how to handle it or what to do with it and more often than not, they don't know how to receive it, but that doesn't stop them from going after it. Moreover, once they find even a trace of it in your spirit, they put you to work on them. Those girls saw what I thought I was hiding. Through everything, they saw compassion.

Scarlet Letter

I wear it
Like the Scarlet Letter
For all to see
The Hester Preen in me
Like she
I choose forbidden love
Not to be defiant
As some may have thought
I've always been reliant
On the murmurings of
My soul
And if truth be told
Never even considered Eve's
Behavior at the tree
I was just being me.

I wear it
Like the Scarlet Letter
For all to see
Like she
I longed to
Drink his tears
Lusted to have him near
Pressed past all my fears
To stand alone
With lights shone bright
I faced the nights
I died a million deaths
I cried a million days
Wrapped in spectacle
I lay
Wrapped in spectacle
I prayed
Listening to the murmurings of
My soul
In all honesty
Though present
He was never there with me

I wear it
Like the Scarlet Letter
Who else
Could display it better?
Except one that
Sampled outlawed love
And decided it had value
A fire started by two
I knew what loving him
Conveyed
I surely express no regrets
In changing times or
Difference in age
Through thorny thoughts
Deep seeded stares
Hard suspicious glances
Curious glares
He knew I would stay
And stay I did
And stay I have
In hopes, that by chance
My love meant more than
Punishment for being smitten and
Like the soft murmuring of a kitten
I listened to my soul.

So, Yes, I wear it
Like the Scarlet Letter
Without complaint
Or looking back
No way to hide
What is plainly seen
Connecting hearts are
Always keen
At navigating
On roads less traveled
Though thick and bumpy,
Laced with gravel
Both myself and
Hester Preen
Did what we thought well.

And So It Began

And so it began, I went out and purchased the book that had helped me break the chains of abuse in my own personal life. The book is titled, *Men Who Hate Women and the Women Who Love Them by Susan Forward and Joan Torres.* I had about four girls meet with me every other day. I gave each one their own copy. I assigned a coupled of chapters at a time, then I met with them to discuss the issues raised through reading. We met during my prep, which is a time set aside everyday for teachers to plan. I also arranged for us to meet after school, and or via the telephone in order to ensure that the girls would get the most out of our lessons. I thought I had covered all bases. It was impossible for them to miss any sessions because I built in ample time for us to meet. Well, as hard as I planned, it turned out to be quite a task to not only get all the girls together but also to discourage them from missing sessions.

It was something new everyday. One girl was pregnant, and she had to miss sometimes because of prenatal appointments. Another girl had a class during my prep; therefore, I had to arrange with the teacher for her to be released. Another girl had lunch and sometimes they would not let her out of the lunchroom on time, and the final girl was in one of the other schools located inside our building. Whoa!

Even when I spoke with them, I never knew what to expect until the session started. Sometimes it would be a group discussion while other times it would be one-on-one. In terms of mentoring, it did not matter. I still had to stay committed. Once the mentee notices that you lose focus when they lose focus, your mentoring is up for grabs. I had to set the standard if anyone was going to grow.

Believe me, there were many days when I just felt like quitting, especially on those occasions when no one showed up or when they showed up without the book. I would just sit there and think to myself, *I gave up my prep for this? They don't even value this.* I felt as though they could have at least sent a message through another student that they couldn't make it—then I could have worked on some of my other responsibilities instead of just sitting there looking silly. The worst things that I thought, I can't even write here. There were a couple of times when I was boiling mad, and I had to just fight back the tears.

One would think that they would have come and checked on me or sent an apologetic message. That was never the case In fact, to my amazement, when they knew that I was angry with them or feeling discouraged, they would either duck the issue or duck me. I discovered in the midst of my own despair, frustration, and fury that I even had to teach them how to apologize.

That is what my mentoring looked like on a bad day, but on a good day, I could see a light bulb turn on. I could hear a pin drop as they listened, and I knew that they were thinking and that always led to some of the best questions, for example, "What is good sex?" or "Can abusers ever get better?" or "Am I stupid because I miss him sometimes?" Questions like those produced the most exciting and insightful discussions. They were universal questions. Questions every woman at some point has had to at least ponder. I loved their questions because not only were they smart and reflective but they also leveled the playing field. I was no longer an adult woman mentoring.

At times, I saw myself as just a girl, like them, trying to make sense of loving men in this world. Of course, I had a larger experience base to pull from, but there were times when that did not make a huge difference. I could just relate to them and them to me. On those occasions, our discussions would be so intense that we would actually get angry when the bell rang, signaling that it was time to go to another class. I lived for those moments. You have to as a mentor. They don't come that often, but when they do, it is magical. You know something magical is happening when you walk away having learned as much as the young people that you are mentoring.

It is hard investing in other people's kids. With your own children, you are with them enough that you get an opportunity to get a sneak-peek at their growth. You can literally watch them when they are not looking. My husband and I do it all the time. Just when we thought we were fed up with one of our kids, we would look up and see that something had clicked inside their spirit. They had changed. They were not only ready to handle more but they also requested the opportunity to do so. With your mentee, many times you just can't tell. It's like wearing a pair of glasses that distort your vision. When you look through them, you know that something is "over there," you just cannot quite make it out.

I wasn't sure what my mentees got from those original mentoring sessions. After all, three continued to date their abuser, and the girl that was an incest survivor continued to live at home with her mom and her abuser. She rationalized that the abuse had ended, and she still wanted a relationship with her mom. I could not understand her choice, but I respected her decision. I did share with her that living there would not build her self-esteem or lead to healing because she was being re-victimized everyday. She said she understood, but I knew she didn't.

With the other girls, just as statistics show, the abuse escalated. I spent more nights than I care to mention listening and crying and getting angry. Sometimes their stories would push me into small bouts of depression. Other times, I would vow that I didn't want to work with them any longer because they didn't want to get better. It's funny how every time I tried to throw one of them away, they would miraculously improve in some area. It was almost as if they could sense in my spirit that I was giving up on them, and they were not about to let me do that. In the end, I could always sleep because I knew that I had done the best that I could. I had to accept something that farmers have long known, which is before one can expect a harvest, one has to plant, water, and tend to the seeds.

True Security

True security knows that
The sun rises each morning
On little girls with toes that
Look like miniature sausages
That toddle out of bed
Eagerly awaiting
The start of their day

True security realizes that
When you don't have enough money
To buy half the things you want
You purchase half the things you need

True security adjusts to
One man's touch and scent
Even when you're invited to sample
31 flavors

It's calling friends that you
Haven't spoken with in
What seems like ages and
Fitting into their life with
The same ease that a baby
Snuggles into Mom's breast

It's wearing your favorite gown
With the hole and
Still feeling refreshed.
It believes that you look great
Even after you've put on weight

It's sitting among
The supposed "pretty people"
And recognizing that
You're the "Beautiful One"
It's cutting off your hair

Just because you feel like it
And not looking for approval

It's kissing the ugly boy
Because he says "you're special"
It's holding hands
With your husband in church
When all the church hags
Have their sanctified noses
Turned up as high as
Their skirts used to be

It's the dog that
Waits by the door
Occasionally sniffing
For your scent
Because they are sure
That you are coming
Home to feed them.

True security is LOVE
All fuzzy and sticky
Light like cotton candy
It encourages little boys
To leap confidently into
Their Dad's arms without
Even considering that
He might drop them

501c3 and Me

I spent virtually my whole summer preparing for the introduction of Purple Rain. I created a logo, registered our official name with the state, had my website built, wrote my 501c3 document, put together a newsletter, created business cards, brochures, and I even had T-shirts made. It was important to me to have everything in place that I would need to give Purple Rain a great kick off by the start of the school year. I was under no illusions. I knew that I was the engine, the sole force willing to move Purple Rain forward. Everyone, except for my husband, made it clear that they were only interested in being the caboose. By the middle of the year, none of the original people with whom I had shared my vision were even interested in being on the tracks. I would discover the toughest lesson yet: the people who had expressed great interest in helping me build Purple Rain were no longer interested—except for my husband. It was amazing. I couldn't even get them to come together for a board meeting. Everyone had an excuse. I even suggested that we try meeting via video conferencing; they told me all kinds of things about the health of their computers. They didn't have an Internet connection, they wouldn't agree on a time. It just got silly.

The greatest insult came from the very woman that had gotten me into this mess in the first place. She was the one who encouraged me to take what I was doing out of my living room and make it into a foundation. She was the one that talked to me about getting charitable status and seeking funding from others. She was the one who gave me ideas about building a board of directors. But once I actually started doing those things, and she saw that I was serious and driven, I barely heard from her. She never even checked on

our progress, and in the end, she didn't even bother to make a donation. Once the rage settled, I had to figure out a way not to completely hate her. I didn't understand her. I still don't. I concluded that she was phony and dishonest. I learned that she was a control freak. It was almost like she saw me as some project, and once she found out that I was a leader and a visionary, she became turned off. I remember when we first sat down for our series of talks. I came home and told my husband that I felt like she was spoon-feeding me information. I could never just get her to tell me everything. She would discuss a little with me and then tell me to come back. I kept thinking, "I'm a grown woman with a Masters Degree. You don't need to treat me as though my brain has a limited capacity to store information."

After our third discussion, I had enough, I just went to the bookstore and purchased everything I could about how to start a not-for-profit organization. It didn't take me long to put the missing pieces of the puzzle together. Once I learned what she had been withholding from me, I was infuriated. The thing that hurt me the most was when I asked her how long she thought it would take me to get my 501c3 status and she told me two years.

I asked her, "Based off what?" She said it was going to take me at least that long to get the document completed and approved by the IRS. In actuality, it only took me six months. I learned a great lesson from her: there is a big difference between sympathy towards an issue vs. empathy. Although she felt pity and sorrow for the girls that I was seeking to service, she was unable to transfer her own feelings and emotions towards them. She was a professional and a "good church going woman." She was the first one in and the last one out. She was proud to tithe her 10%. She was active in their hospitality ministry, and at one point she even recruited my husband and I to help in that capacity. We didn't do it long because it didn't allow us to use any of our gifts. She showed me that if Purple Rain was to exist, it would have to come from me—and so it did.

Mentors have to be careful that they do not let slackers, naysayers, and saboteurs become a distraction. Much of the mission is achieved alone. Many times, it takes some getting used to the loneliness, the disappointment, and bouts of discouragement. However, when you accept the deck that you are dealt and you keep a close watch on the players, you still have an opportunity to win. The reality is that most mentoring starts with one person taking the time to pour their life into another's. Anything that happens beyond that is the icing on the cake.

I ASK THE IMPOSSIBLE

I ask the impossible when
I look into my kids' eyes
After hearing them say
Something silly and I quietly
Without them knowing
Pray to God that he never
Take me from them

I don't want to miss
Goofy Jokes
Tales of betrayal
First kisses
First fights
First makeups
And forever friends

I don't want to miss
Terrible hair days
Ugly outfits
I want to stay to
Poke fun at
New boyfriends and
Former girlfriends

They need me!
To be around to
Side with them
To say, "He looks like he stank
Date someone else."
And "I didn't like that heifer anyway"
Who else will fuss with them?
Or about them
Like I do?

Surely, they can't find anyone
That knows them better.
I've known them
From day one.

I remember
Missed periods
Puff to egg
Round belly changes
Ultra sound excitement
Warm water bag bursts

I ask the impossible when
I look into their eyes and
I wish I could transfer
The joy I experienced when
They were night owls and chatterboxes
When I could get them
To behave by pretending
That I was speaking to their
Favorite cartoon character
On the phone.

I want to stay with them forever.
I want them to feel the same about me.
I hope that they always remember all
The silly names that I have called them
"Teffy Weffy Puddin and Pie"
"Big Toe Burger"
"Langston Fee Fy Foe Fangston
Master of Stankston"

I hope.
Besides, why wouldn't they?
Who's to say?
After all, I made it through
Sleepy impossible mornings
Ran into tired impossible nights that
Slowly, without me noticing
Reshaped itself into a
Mother's joy and ultimately a
Plea to God not to
Take me from my children
I want to be with them forever
Maybe, LOVE has made that request
Not so, impossible, after all

Once School Started

Once school started, I announced to all the students in my class that I had a website, and shared with them my purpose and goal in it's development. You would have had to be a fly on the wall to really understand just how strange many of the students looked at me. They really couldn't believe that I even had my own website much less that it was actually built to support girls being beat up by their boyfriends. I think they thought that if I was going to have a website, it should be about something cool like music or fashion. I can be an intense person; therefore, they didn't have any choice but to take me seriously, which helped capture their interest in the cause.

I was surprised at the number of girls who expressed interest in checking out Purple Rain. Thirty-three girls signed up to receive additional information about my club. Many girls stayed after class to explain that they weren't personally being beaten up but that they had witnessed their best friends, or sisters, and in many cases their moms getting abused. They made me promise that I would let them know when we would be having our first meeting. I actually had not thought that far ahead, but their interest forced
the next step. You can never predict what will ignite young people's interest, but once you have it, you had better have something to say that will engage it.

I planned my first meeting in September on a half school day. I had a teacher that is famous for making incredible cakes make "kick-off" cake, in the shape of my logo. I did a short presentation and gave out a copy of the current newsletter and a letter of intent that essentially laid out the expectations of the club. I was sure to include a student and parent agreement section with a place for a signature. The experience was more than exciting—it was exhilarating. It's always fun to be innovative, but it's even more incredible to know that you are going to be changing people's lives. I knew that Purple Rain was going to do that. What was happening was unheard of—an actual support group for teen girls inside the school being sponsored and run by a teacher.

Normally, when inner-city schools offer support to young people, they bring in consultants. Consultants lack the history and personal connections with the student/community base. They also lack complete knowledge of that particular school's culture and climate. Honestly, I've watched them come and I've watched them go. They don't stay because they don't have to. Once they have utilized their entire curriculum, the grant runs out, or the school decides to reallocate space, they leave, and most times the youth feel abandoned. Hurting or disenfranchised youth never want positive adults to leave their lives. That is why it's important to help them learn to heal so that they don't feel empty and lost. It also aids them in understanding the cycle of life, love, and friendship while teaching them to rely on their own inner strength. In reality, we can't keep everyone with us that we love, but they are forever ingrained in our hearts.

It's funny that when you are planning, you just don't consider certain things. I knew that launching Purple Rain was going to be a lot of work, but I hadn't really considered just how difficult it might be to manage my normal activities—like grading papers, cooking, doing homework with my own kids, or even just sitting down to enjoy a show with my husband.

In the beginning, I was managing things fine. I had a once a week meeting, we did a service learning project, and an outside activity. Initially that was easy to handle, but later on, it became more of a challenge. In order to give Purple Rain legs, I had to give Purple Rain me. I allowed it to consume my every thought and action. I even dreamt about it. I had to use every skill known to man, including those that lend themselves into the psychic realm. I'm not trying to get too deep, but there were moments when my planning, and organizing, and leading required me to see things unseen by the natural eye. I had to believe. I just had to know. Besides, there was no turning back now. I had set the bar high, and I did not intend to let go.

Mentors have to set the standard and remain the ultimate coach/motivator. They must accept that when things go right, they will receive modest acknowledgement. However when things go wrong, they will get the full blame. They must prepare for that dichotomy. They must press through the fog with a complete belief that storm clouds usually settle and open to sunshine.

IT WAS JUST A SHIRT

It was just a shirt
When I first saw it
I thought of him
I could just see how
Incredible he was going to look
When he walked into the office

The shirt had this strong
 Middle Eastern flair while
Keeping an Urban feel
Some people make the clothes
Some clothes make the people
It seemed to me that they would
Compliment each other

I ordered it
And eagerly awaited
The mail carrier's delivery
I thought to myself, "they got a lot of opinions about what
Ebony men look good in but this shirt would
Surely put a stop to that talk at least for that day."

It arrived.
And the shirt looked better than
When it was in the catalogue
He was so excited and proud
I said, "You have to save that and whip it out on a special occasion."
He smiled in agreement.

He couldn't wait to try it on.
And I couldn't wait to see him in it.
When he put it on,
He looked so fine.

I could tell that he felt good about himself
'Cause he just strutted in it.
He even did a double take in the mirror.

Nothing makes a woman feel better
Than doing something that pleases
Her man and I was delighted to have pleased him.

It was just a shirt
But my heart had went into
Every inch of that gift
I saw him
I saw him with me
I saw us
Out enjoying things
I saw sweet glances
I saw intrigued stares
I saw envious glares
Our joy together
Would be the "who cares."

One day, I sat on the porch
Enjoying the summer air
When he arrived home with
The shirt strewn over his shoulder
I was taken by surprise
I can't even explain why?
But it bugged me
And I couldn't let it go

I asked with irritation in my voice
"Why do you have your shirt off?"
Not really making good eye contact

He replied, "I got hot plus I didn't want to get it real wrinkled"

Like the start of a Maytag Washer
My stomach churned
Like the heat that rises from a
Smoldering barbeque pit
My insides burned
When I looked at him
I couldn't help but think
How much he reminded me
Of the pigs at a pig stall,
Feeding on a mixture of food and their own shit.
The only difference was
He was trying to feed
It to me.

When our eyes finally locked
He knew that I knew
And I knew that he knew I knew
But I couldn't prove anything

I never liked that shirt after that
And he didn't enjoy
Wearing it any longer
On a couple of occasions
After that incident
He put it on and
I acted as if I didn't even notice it
Blank, cold stares of indifference
Landed the shirt in a permanent position in the back of the closet
Where it hung limply with all
Its secrets sweated inside
Each strand of its fiber

The same way
Shame was pressed deep into
The fiber of me.
It was just a shirt
When I saw it
I thought of him
I still do.

Premier Club

Without a doubt, Purple Rain became the premier club at AASTA High School. We were active inside as well as outside the campus. Each month, we organized a service-learning project that ranged from collecting teddy bears to give to the littlest victims of domestic violence to raising money for the victims of the Tsunami. I developed a relationship with a professor at Columbia College, and she graciously brought 25 of her college students over to our high school campus in order to allow the girls to participate in the Clothesline Project, which is a display of t-shirts that reflect the pain felt about the violence men direct towards women and girls.

When we weren't being humanitarians, we were learning about culture; and when we weren't learning about culture, we were participating in workshops; and when we weren't participating in workshops, we were reading and writing. Our lists of activities were endless because my husband and I put great effort in finding and securing solid partnerships. We recognized from the very beginning that we needed to align ourselves with other groups and/or organizations—people who had a heart for working with at-risk youth. We dreamed so hard for the group and even harder for the girls. We could not function in a vacuum if we were going to be successful; we needed additional support and resources.

What do you do when you don't have access to multimedia equipment? Find a youth organization that does and see if they are willing to work with your youth. How do you expose your youth to more culture? Find other groups that put on dance, music, and art displays for little to no cost. How do you help develop individual strengths? Locate other organizations that have programs in place that your youth can be plugged into. Our partnerships offered us all of those options without carrying tremendous overhead or having to write endless grants. They allowed us to focus most of our energy on distributing information, organizing transportation, and mentoring.

It has always been my belief that young people, particularly young women, stay trapped in negative situations because they begin to see it as something to do, a way of belonging, a type of activity. Keeping that in mind, I made it my mission to ensure that members in my club "could get in where they fit in." In other words, there was something in place for everyone. Every club wants 100% participation, but realistically in high school that is almost impossible. All it takes is a young person to fall behind on their assignments or have a confrontation with a parent or become unable to secure a babysitter and their level of involvement will diminish. I knew from being a teacher in the classroom what obstacles I would face in that area, which is why I set up three levels of membership. They were as follows:

1. **Members** attended meetings, workshops, and events at least 80% of the time.
2. **Associate members** attended meetings, workshops, and events at least 50% of the time.
3. **Friends** of Purple Rain attended meetings, workshops, and events rarely due to things out of their control, but they continued to express sincere interest in the mission of the group.

One would think that the three levels of membership would guarantee regular attendance and a clear commitment. After all, the girls had room to shift within levels without losing membership status. To my surprise, it did not guarantee anything. In fact, sometimes it caused confusion. Not because the system was confusing but rather because the girls were resistant to seeing themselves as less committed than other girls. They felt as though once they expressed interest and showed up to one event or participated in one fundraiser that they were in firm. They didn't really see why I made such a big deal about missed activities or meetings. They wanted me to accept that the mere fact that they supported the cause meant that they were members of the group.

In order to become a premier club, I had to tear down that thinking. I could not allow that mindset to breed. The members make up any club and you can't be a club if the members don't show up. It is difficult to teach young people to value the investment that mentors put into them. They struggle to respect the time that mentors take away from their own families, friends, and personal interests. Sometimes, they don't even view the mentor as having feelings. It is disappointing to organize an event or have another group set aside space or tickets for your members only to discover that they have no intention of showing up. The "no shows" are one thing, but the lack of consideration that usually accompanies that behavior is another. I can't tell you the number of times that my mentees stood me up without even bothering to call and inform me. I usually found out once I parked outside the school waiting for them to arrive. I learned a lot about the differences between our value systems. They taught me that they didn't see time as precious even though most of my mentees hurt over the lost

or lack of time that adults or significant others weren't willing to give up in order to sincerely share in successes and deal with their failures.

Mentors have to teach their youth that there is honor in sacrifice and that their words must be their bonds. If we do not, what remains is a bunch of people too busy to stop and genuinely care. I wanted us to be a premier club, different from everyone else, our bond cemented. To achieve that, I had to have a system that would protect the flowers from the weeds and the three levels helped me do that, or so I thought.

I Come From

I come from a mix of
Gary Indiana and Augusta Georgia
From thick black molasses and
The hunting of wild game
From soft moonlit nights and
Hours of laying and lying and
Telling lies in order to hide the truth
A truth that is ever present
Even though it seems ever past.

I come from sassy rule breaking hours
That ran into Robust rule breaking days
That limped into back breaking nights
I come from her who
Received him
In passionate exchanges
Green-eyed glances
Deep pillow talk moments
Kitchen chat deception
Bellowing cries and
Pressure cooked outbursts

I come from late night fights
That bleed outside the borders of reason
Causing me to ask Why I come from them?
Did I have to travel through lawless loins
To be birthed from people that
Eat greens and cornbread with their fingers

I come from huge altercations
Preposterous forgiveness
Committed love
Committed hate
I come from drums
That beat on
Walls of deception
That sat on
Rugs of secrets

Listen,
Take hold
Watch a Maverick
A wild stallion

Protected under
God's shield of Grace
Extending love
Pretending to be
Things Tall
Things Good
In silence and shock
Shock in silence
Sometimes laced
In confusion
Trapping purple El Dorado dreams
When riding "shot gun"
Took the place of Amusement parks
Proving beaming hours sheds its suit
When it's ready, it dresses up as
Glistening days and
When it stops looking "sugar sharp"
From too many washings
My sun presses through
Dull memories,
Listless nights,
Old harbored fears
It evaporates tears

It shines on positive spaces
In once dark places
Reminding me that even
Concrete jungles hold
A lot of fun
Reminding me how
Sliding boards
Use to burn like hell
Under the hot
Summer sun but
I still could not wait
To get on it

Yeah, I come from a mix of
Gary Indiana and Augusta Georgia
Thick black molasses and
The hunting of wild game
I am reminded everyday
That mix
Ain't a bad blend
After all.

Pulling Weeds

What are weeds? Generally, the term weed is used to describe any plant that is unwanted and grows or spreads aggressively. Looks can be deceiving. To many, invasive weeds are simply beautiful wildflowers and some of them, such as purple loosestrife or wisteria, are favored by gardeners for their beauty and hardiness, but when allowed to escape into wild lands, they cause serious ecological and economic damage to many areas.

I had no idea just how hard it would be to encourage the young women to take ownership of their club, to exercise using their minds and their voices, to step forward as leaders outside the club and within the ranks. Many of them just didn't want to separate themselves from their friends—even when it was clear that the positive activities in which they were involved through Purple Rain were changing their lives. I lost the opportunity to mentor many young women because they allowed their friendships to supersede their growth.

I remember taking all of the girls who had created a t-shirt for the Clothesline Project over to Colombia College for the closing of the exhibit. We had essentially made history. Twenty-six young black women, many of who were not even Purple Rain members, had designed and displayed t-shirts that exposed the truth about rape, incest, and abuse. Their display had riveted the school and awakened many of their own souls. The project itself was a coming together of high school and college, black and white, low income, and middle class. Our union crossed so many lines, yet it connected every dot. It was unmistakably important and undeniably heard. Yet, when I took them over to Columbia as the featured guests, instead of taking their time to view the exhibit, admire one another's work, and take in the experience, many of them sat at the table joking about the latest gossip at the school. I even had to chastise a few girls for cracking jokes on the passing college students.

The most difficult part of the experience was watching Purple Rain girls with whom I had spoken with about their own abuse participate in that negative behavior. When I confronted them, almost all of them admitted that they were acting that way because they were "just tripping" with their friends, as if we were on some social outing. I had to nip that negativity in the bud. They knew why we were there. They went in understanding the expectation, yet they laughed as their shirts hung, revealing sadness so deep one would need a shovel to dig it up and a U-Haul truck to take it away. I made up my mind that day that I would "weed and feed." In other words, I would never bring a girl to an event of that nature unless they had demonstrated clear growth because of mentoring. I learned that day that Purple Rain needed intense work in the area of self-love and self-respect. I am sure the Columbia people didn't notice most of it, but I knew and it broke my heart to see just how quickly the weeds spread and dominated the flowers.

Mentors cannot be afraid to separate their mentees from their friends and their social set. They must accept that they will not reach every young person that comes through the door. Many do not even want to be mentored. Their job is always to find the "one red rose among the weeds," and with the best of their abilities, protect and nurture it so that it can grow.

Induction Ceremony

By December, only 11 out of the 33 girls who had originally expressed interest in Purple Rain had emerged as serious participants. They were active in our book club, attending workshops, involved themselves in service learning projects, wrote for our web journal and newsletter, and helped with fundraising. I could even depend on most of their families for support. Some of their parents attended events and assisted me with transportation. There was great communication between us and among us. They knew my expectations, and they seemed to want to live up to them. I was proud of them, and I wanted to honor their preliminary commitment; therefore, I decided to have an Induction Ceremony.

The Induction Ceremony was a symbolic start to their membership. It was a declaration of their commitment, service, and retention. It was a dignified event that lent itself to keeping new members interested and engaged while acknowledging that they were valuable to the club. It was understood that inductees would receive thoughtful follow through and a more intense and meaningful orientation to the group. I wanted these young women to have an evening where they completely shined. I wanted to announce not only to the school but also to the world that these were my Purple Rain Girls. "Others may claim it, but they were named it."

The exact details of the evening are unimportant, after all, the Induction Ceremony is more for the inductees than the onlookers.

I think that it suffices to say that the girls looked beautiful and that the highlight of the evening was reading the poems that I had written for each inductee, which detailed those things that made them special in my heart and demonstrated why I thought their membership would strengthen the fiber of Purple Rain. Without saying for whom the poems had been written, each girl had to figure it out by listening. The same way that I had discovered them, they had to discover themselves through lyrical verse. Without a doubt, it was an enchanting evening, full of hope and promise. I felt elated. I was confident that I had assembled a caring, thoughtful, and focused team open to the mentoring process, excited about further developing leadership skills, and comfortable with healing personal scars. I had a lot to learn, and no one could have prepared me for what was looming. As is life's way, she chose to reveal her hand to me when she was ready, but that night I danced content with believing that we were ready for the next level, solid in my commitment to get us there.

Mentors should organize some kind of rite of passage ceremony. How they structure it is entirely up to them. Whether creative or conservative, they should just have one. It will give their youth a reason to work hard while acknowledging their dedication and most of all; it bonds and builds camaraderie among group members.

Purple Pledge

Because I believe, that Purple Rain is only as good
As its members' commitment to grow, change,
And support one another, I pledge:

To work everyday to remember that
I am a valuable person inside and out and
I don't have to accept abuse of any kind

To practice letting go of negative feelings
And behaviors that I have kept pent up
And that have hindered my growth

To no longer allow fear to keep me
From expressing the violence that
I have either seen or experienced

To utilize every chance to express
My feelings about abuse in hopes of
Breaking the cycle of violence for the next generation

To actively work to support members,
Other women, and girls that may be
Experiencing similar struggles

To no longer give any abuser
A platform to control me
By keeping their secrets

To use my voice to expose him and
His behavior for what it really is
Anti-Woman, Anti-Love, and Anti-God

<u>Special Note</u>

As a mentor, I recognize that working with minors adds a level of complication as it applies to confidentiality issues. Although this is my memoir, I did not want to share anything about a young person that would cause them to feel embarrassed, humiliated, or ashamed—thus I have changed the name of each mentee that I reference to the name of a flower that can be found in different shades of purple.

Violet

I just like you
It's as simple as that
-No complicated
Explanations needed
-No long exaggerated
Consonant or vowel sounds
To draw the listener in
-No need to use the
Thesaurus or pull out the
Dictionary to double check
The definition. I know my
Feelings
I'm sure that
I like you.

You are a
Modern day "Coffee Brown"
Pretty and Powerful
You don't take no stuff
Off of anyone, but you still
Know how to love
And besides,
I like your Toffee Sweet favor
Natural Beauty
Like Princess Diana
The camera loves you
The paparazzi follow you
But, I'm blessed to know
You
And call you "Friend"

Iris

It's funny how some people you meet
You just like upon first sight
And others have to grow on you.
It's like finding these awesome shoes
In your size and once you place your
Feet in them, you realize that they
Need to be stretched.
Instantly, there is this emotional
Tug of War
That goes on inside the mind
Should I get them?
Nawh, it makes more sense to find
Something else that's a perfect fit.

This is the best way that I can
Describe our relationship.
We are not a "perfect fit"
However, the Tug of War is over
And we have decided to
Stretch

Our minds
Our time
Most importantly,
Our friendship

I've come to see
The beauty in the cantankerous
Nature of
A moody teen
Who in spite of our initial
Rolling of eyes and
Smacking of lips and
Sneaky irritated glances
Has found favor in me

I've come to see the beauty in
the defiant
Nature of a young woman that
has enough
"Chutzpah" to say "I'm not doing
that"
I've come to see the beauty in
Quiet eyes that leak disapproval
Over issues that rub her wrong

You are strong and loyal and
kind
I'm proud that I took the time
To fight through the Tug of War
And Stretch myself more
Giving space for us to grow
Into one another

We are not a "perfect fit"
But we are perfect friends.

Wildflower

We used to sit
Across
Sometimes near
Never far
From one another
In a circle of girls
Lead by the
Goddess of Narcissism
"Let's do our Girl's Pledge"
"I am a girl"
"I am an expression of
Beauty, joy, and love."

Blah, Blah, Blah, Blah

For weeks, we were
Supposedly bonding
You know,
Becoming Sisters or
At least reluctant friends
For sure, we were required
To pretend
Although, none of us
Ever really believed it

See, because true relations
Require some kind of Relationship
You know, like,
I get to know you and
You get to know me.
The process is simple
Even in its complication.

We used to sit
Across
From one another
In fact, I even remember an
Occasion or two
When, after completing our pledge

"I am a girl"
"I am growing into a woman"
"I am it"
"I am the joy the world is
waiting for!"

That we actually had an
opportunity to talk about real
stuff like life, love, boys, why
you were crying by the
lockers?
Only to be interrupted, once
again, by a voice, an irritating
voice at that, giving group
direction.
"Let's check back in"
"Okay, who wants to talk first?"

Deep Sighs
Uncomfortable glances
Quick looks away
"I'll go"
Blah, Blah, Blah, Blah.

Done
With pseudo-girl groups
We've started our own
Where we regularly sit
Across
Sometimes near
Never far
From one another
In a circle of girls
And sometimes simply
One on one
Led by our combined
Passion for Purple and More

I can finally say what I wanted
To say then
You are beautiful, sweet, and
bubbly and I'm glad that we
are friends.

28

Magnolia

Like the Breeze that arises
From the lakefront after a hot
July day
You are just what's needed to
Keep things copasetic

That is-
Calm and Cool
You're neither
Fire nor ice
Shy or bold
You just know
How to hold
Your own

One of the few
That can talk
About your faith
And what it does
For you
While explaining
The meaning of your
Name-
You raise the game or
Should I say the bar?

You don't do
What they do
In the hallways
And classrooms

You don't
Participate in
Negative climate changing
Behavior

You know better
And you do better
Having been blessed
At birth with a name that
Would describe your
Essence
Define your steps

In Arabic you are
Righteous
In Islam you are Wise or
Mature
In Pakistan you are a
Beautiful Flower
The description is not for
an hour
It is for life

Continue to follow the
footsteps of old as you
navigate the patterns of
new.

Lilac

Your warmth is like heat
Rising from an oven
Filled with the sweet scent
Of Gingerbread
Nice.
To know
Easy
Like Sunday morning sleep-ins
Giving comfort and Joy
At the same time.

Your warmth is like the sun
After a cool dip
In the pool,
Relieving tension
Taking away
Damp quivers
Forcing smiles
From what was
Once concrete cheeks

See, behind
The little stature
Carefully brushed ponytail
Small round specs
Is love
And
You are the embodiment to
Love

And seeing that Love is the most
Important verb in the dictionary
It's impossible for you to contain
The cascading warmth that flows
From your heart.

I noticed from the start
Having handed you
My heart in return
Confident
That you would
Handle it with
Care

What exists between us
Will always be there
Our heart connection
Has secured that fact

You warmth is all consuming
Never gloomy and
It radiates on me.

Chrysanthemum

You lace yourself in joy
Allowing the world to share
In your
Silly Grins
Connected to
Warm smiles that
Often rollover into
Sweet chuckles
Reminding one of
Maggie, the baby
In the Simpson's.

You are a neat, nice, delight
To know
You carry a natural glow
That like the florescent light
Slowly warms a room.

You lace yourself in Joy
Allowing Looney Tunes laughs
To lower defensive walls
Leaving space along life's
Boardwalk to smell the roses

Your natural effervescence makes
Knowing you a Hoot
And when you're sad
Even the Sun packs up her
Suitcase and leaves town
Only to return when
She hears the soft crescendo
Of your giggle
Make ripples across the Ocean
Of love
Full of Life
You lace yourself in joy.

Orchid

You were the first
To challenge the
Capacity of my heart
To grow—
Like the Grinch
I sat high, irritated
Looking down
Wondering what all
The fuss was about in
"Whoville" or should I say
"Youville"

You, who sat quiet
Barely able to speak
Avoiding eye contact
Forcing incomplete
Sentences out of an
Half-opened mouth
Making me demand that
You "stop being so
Phony and speak up."

After all, you spoke to him
All the time
As earlier as
When the cock crowed
Until the moon put on his
Nightcap and fell asleep
Expressing sultry, sexual,
Professions of devoted teen
Love that leaked intense longings
Of forever ness, but you said
As little as possible to me.

Until the Apple turned pink
And all the leaves on your
Once sturdy tree
Fell removing all shade
Exposing more than
Sun burned and peeling skin
It exposed the him within
That took pleasure in
Power
Punches and
Pain
Especially as your
Young tummy grew
Then I learned
What all the fuss
In "youville"
Was really all
About.

You were the first
To challenge
My heart
To grow—
I'm glad that
I've made space
Within

Pansy

Would have never thought twice
In fact, eventually, I couldn't even
Remember your name
You
Complicated and Plain
Me
Needing a smile
While
Every time we locked eyes
You looked so bland
Until…
Then-One day
Who can say why?
You looked me in the eye
And
Love locked in
And I do mean love
I found a glimmer of brightness.

A sign of sorrow and joy
Laced in teen confusion
Looking for Guidance
Extending
A hand
And I reached
Out and
Your fingers locked with mine
I knew
We knew
That we were friends

No words needed
That's not your style
But you did give me
That much needed smile

33

Loosestrife

They can say
What they want but
Every now and again
You meet
Your twin

Identical
Fraternal
Irish or
Just plain
Similar in Spirit

You are
Principled
Cynical
Optimistic
Cuss
Capable of giving
Your own self
A hug

You are vocal
Not to be confused with a
Vocalist-
Simply exercising
Your vocal cords as
Part of a performance'

You have, in fact, something
To say and
They know it and
They listen to
Your
Loud
Lyrical
Professions
Of a teenage drama stopper
Wrapped in tomboyish gear

Spunk or should I say drive
You are a natural leader
With an ability to sort
Truth from fiction
Fiction from fantasy
Fantasy from dreams
All the while
Pulling the grade and
Posting pictures of
Lloyd Banks on your
Bedroom wall.

Petunia

They say never judge a book by its cover
And I've learned that's good advice
Seeing that I've had an opportunity to read
The words inside
You-
Taught me that
Behind
The little glasses
Thin ponytail and
Ole fashion demeanor
Lives
Sweetness
Not like Walter Payton
Although you are just
As committed as he was
To football
Not like cookies
Although knowing you
Is a treat
Not like Sugar
Although just adding
You in, decreases the tart in
Our hearts
But rather like Honey
Natural, Medicinal, and good for the
Body and the mind
Acknowledged all over the world as
Having Value
Even though the bees that labor to create it
Seem never to even notice.
However, I notice you
And I've learned never judge a book by its
Cover because....
You just might miss the beautiful
Story within

Wisteria

You are a
Big Brown Bear
Batting eyelashes
While flashing teeth
Connected to a
Wide grin
That draws
Us in

You are a
Beautiful Blue Bird
Bumping hips or
Rather thoughts
With those
Who relate to
Your comedic moments

You are a
Bright Brilliant Butterfly
Fluttering with ease
Among many
Who view Butterflies as bugs
Something to be ignored or
Stamped out.

I say, strut on "Lady Love"
Continue to be the Sharpest Lady Bug of
them
All.
They can't rain on your parade
Especially when you're
Felling good
Adorned with your
Polka Dot Fedora
Slightly cocked over
Your left eye

"Baby Bye"

Pruning Flowers

Proper pruning enhances the beauty of almost any landscape tree and shrub. Pruning, like any other skill, requires knowing what you are doing to achieve success. The old idea that anyone with a chainsaw or a pruning saw can be a landscape pruner is far from the truth. More trees are killed or ruined each year from improper pruning than by pests. Pruning is the removal or reduction of certain plant parts that are not required, that are no longer effective, or that are of no use to the plant. It is done to supply additional energy for the development of flowers, fruits, and limbs that remain on the plant.

As stated earlier, no one could have prepared me for what was looming. I had no idea the level of disappointment and utter frustration that was awaiting me. The weeks that followed the Induction Ceremony made me question my methods, my choices, and my decisions. How could something that was so right dissolve into something so shabby? I thought I had put everything in place to ensure that Purple Rain would succeed. Yet, like the Ibo culture described in the book *Things Fall Apart,* by Chinua Achebe, it was as if our group was held together by one string—and although the string had not broken, it was being pulled, which was forcing it to unravel, causing everything it held together to literally fall apart.

The first sign of trouble was when my inductee named *Magnolia* arrived at our regular Thursday meeting with a friend. I really didn't have a problem with that because they usually left school together. Prior to the meeting starting, I needed to run to the office to make a Xerox. I was gone all of five minutes and when I returned, *Magnolia* had left. The girls informed me that as soon as I walked out of the room, she simply looked at her friend and said, "Do you want to go?

Well, let's go," and they left. I was actually shocked. She had been one of my faithful attendees. I had been to her church, met her mother and grandmother—in fact, her mother had encouraged her to be a part of our writers workshop.

When I got home that evening, I called her and asked her why she had left. I quoted back to her what the girls described her as saying before she left. She didn't deny it. She just kept speaking rude and nonchalant to me. She said, "I had to go." I asked her why she didn't just say that prior to the meeting, and she had no answer. I asked her when did we start treating one another that way, and she just repeated that she had to go. She wasn't even willing to extend an apology. I informed her that I wasn't going to bother her any longer. I said let me know when you are serious.

Her infraction may seem minor; however, the other girls were looking to see how I was going to handle it and depending on how I handled it, was going to make a difference in how they treated meeting attendance. I had to nip that in the bud. If you are an inducted member and you treat meetings that way, what were we to expect of newcomers? *Magnolia* never returned, and I never asked her to. I simply continued to work with the mentees that stayed consistent.

The second set of fallouts centered on the three members who had children. They struggled not only to attend meetings but also to attend everything else. During the school day, they could get involved in some things but anything that required extracurricular commitment was out of the question. I tried everything to keep them involved. I gave *Lilac* a computer because she had a baby and she was married. My thoughts were that she could at least be involved with our group online and that she could write articles for our newsletter. *Lilac* never purchased Internet service, and it took her about one month to write an essay about how she'd survived domestic violence, which was unusable. *Chrysanthemum and Orchid* always had an excuse, and most of it centered on baby-sitting or transportation issues. On many occasions, I would offer them a ride but more often than not, they still couldn't attend. Even though their parents agreed to allow them to be involved with Purple Rain, and they claimed to appreciate my investing in their daughters, they wouldn't support their involvement. Their families began to function as saboteurs, literal roadblocks to their success. I never understood how they could have pregnant and abused teenage daughters, and not assist any adult willing to work with them. Nevertheless, they did not.

For a short time, in an effort to support *Chrysanthemum and Orchid,* I allowed them to bring their babies, but as their babies grew, so did the distractions and the noise. There were moments when the other mentees couldn't even hear themselves think. I finally had to tell them to stay home if they couldn't find a sitter because they weren't going to get anything out of it, and it wasn't fair to the other girls.

Iris, although she never attended our Sunday book club, had been regularly attending events. She was also my best fundraiser, and I had a great relationship with her mother—which was rare. Her mother was so supportive that I wanted her to be in the group. In truth, her mom attended so many events that I made her an honorary member. By the end of February, everything had changed. *Iris* was hanging with a girl who was a truant. The girl had hung around with Purple Rain and in fact, I fully expected her to become a member, but the streets started calling her. Both would skip classes or skip school. Their names floated up as being involved in some sexcapes around the building. I was never close with either of them so when I asked questions, they just denied things and I couldn't prove anything except that they had skipped school or cut classes. Eventually, the school contacted the parents and their behavior was addressed. However, by that time they were no longer invested in PR. The few times that *Iris* came around after that, she acted awkward in her skin. In the frenzy, her relationship with one of the other members, who she had considered a best friend, had faded. This gave her even less reason to come back to the group.

I have always hated the way things played out with *Iris* because I do think that she was growing and that she did love being with us. Besides, we never actually had a falling out; we just had a falling away.

Every group has one, that person who attends everything but who does not help the group grow. PR was no exception. Her name was *Pansy*. My first impression of *Pansy* was that she seemed distant and boring. From her appearance, to her speech, everything reflected low self-esteem. Once I had an opportunity to read a sample of her writing, I knew for sure that I was dealing with a struggling learner. On the other hand, she was nice and quietly enthusiastic. When I organized any event, she was present. I decided that I would give her time. Sometimes, young people are so empty that you have to deposit a lot in their spirit before you get any kind of return. I was willing to do that. The best mentors are. Every month, it was my habit to assess where my mentees were. I believed in keeping a close pulse on their growth. I can honestly say that after several months of interaction, activities, and book club, *Pansy* had grown very little. Her biggest issues centered on communication.

She almost never shared or commented on anything. When asked her opinion about things, she would always reply that she didn't know or that she needed more time to think, but rarely did she give a response. What was most disturbing was the blank stare she kept on her face while people were pouring out their souls. On one irritating occasion, she came to Sunday book club without her book. It was bad enough that she never read or contributed to the discussion but how dare she show up without the book.

Our relationship fractured, on my birthday, when spontaneously, some of the PR girls decided to come to my home and surprise me. She had nothing to do so she tagged along. I have a rule about my birthday. I never go to work because I want to ensure, as much as possible, that it remains a stress and drama free day. I am a bit of a workaholic, so I look forward to that one day when I just let it all roll off. The girls showed up with her, and I immediately felt my heart sink. I just didn't feel like her energy. Many times, she would just sit there like a bump on a log. It is hard to enjoy someone who doesn't have a gift to gab, much less an intellectual bone in their body. On a regular day, I accept where my mentees are and I work with them, but this was my birthday, my one off day.

To make a long story short, we ended up getting into a confrontation over her report card. Besides being my mentee, she was also my Spanish student, and I noticed on her report that the grade she'd received was incorrect. She had received a "C" when it should have been an "F." She and I had already spoken, and I had informed her that she was failing the class. As soon as I alerted her that I would be making a grade correction, she went into a funk. I mean, she literally sat there with her mouth poked out. Nothing the girls did changed her spirits. She even looked that way when the girls began to sing happy birthday. To add insult to injury, she wouldn't even eat any of the cake. At a certain point, I became enraged; I yelled at her, I pounded my fist on the table, and I asked her, "What is wrong with you? Why are you here?" I suggested that she go home, but she didn't budge. She just sat there. I hurried and gave everyone a piece of cake, and I rushed to drop them off at home.

My husband came in on the tail end of everything and asked what had happened. He said that the air was heavy, and I sadly described how I had blown up at *Pansy*. I knew that my relationship with her was forever changed; however, I didn't know to what degree. Occasionally you have a big fight with a youth; you both retreat and think over what just occurred, and when you meet on a later date, you are able to discuss things on a deeper level. When the bond is solid, you are able to listen to one another and come to a place of forgiveness. Unfortunately, this wasn't the outcome for *Pansy* and me. She chose to have her mother call and confront me.

I explained to her mother that I had had several discussions with *Pansy* about her grades, and she was well aware that she was failing the class. Her mom called to argue. She had decided after five months of allowing me to pick her daughter up, pay for events, induct her into the group, and see her home safely that I had it out for her daughter and that I was playing favorites. She decided to call the principal in hopes of blocking the grade change. She informed me that she didn't want her daughter involved with PR any longer. I told her that I had no problem with that.

I came to the meeting prepared: I had samples of *Pansy's* work, her incomplete final exam, pictures that she had given me with inscriptions that expressed how much she cared about me, and copies of tags that she had posted on our group web journal expressing how much she loved being in PR. Even with all of that presented to the parent, her mom still contended that I had it out for her daughter. She wouldn't concede that although I shouldn't have yelled at her daughter, her daughter had been out of line to behave the way she had at my home. After all, her visit was unannounced and she had not been invited. She didn't want to accept that the meeting was less about me having yelled at her daughter and more about her being disappointed that I was going to change her grade to what she had earned.

The mother continued to accuse me of being out to get her daughter and after a while, I became angry and I told her that her problem was that she didn't want to discipline her daughter and that her daughter was a manipulator and liar. I knew the language that I was using was inflammatory. I also knew that I was under attack because of a series of lies that Pansy had told both her mother and me, although for different reasons. I tried not to reveal what Pansy had shared with me in confidence, unfortunately she had tangled me in her web of deception and I knew only the truth would let me out. In order to bring clarity, I asked her mom a series of rhetorical questions, such as, if I've been so terrible to her, why has she shown up at almost every event? Why did she call me over Christmas break to complain about an argument that was happening between you and your brother, and why did she tell me that her grades dropped because she was pregnant?

The mother's mouth fell open because she had been unaware. She could see in her daughter's face that I had spoken the truth. For a minute, she began to chastise her daughter. She told her that she shouldn't be

discussing the things that go on in their home with anyone and then she quickly shifted back to me saying that her daughter couldn't be pregnant because she was using the patch. For further accuracy explained who she said she was pregnant by, what school he attended, and where she claimed that she had gone to have an abortion performed. Once again, she looked at her daughter and she could tell that some of what I was saying had to be true. She told her that they were going to have a nice talk once they got home but like clockwork, she was right back to accusing me of not liking her daughter. The principal finally asked me to leave because the mother and I had locked horns. As I was leaving, the mother told me that it wasn't over and that she was going to call the Board of Education on me. I told her that she could do as she pleased, but she and her daughter were sick.

Within a few days, the principal called me into her office to inform me that *Pansy's* mom had indeed called the Board of Education. My heart sank. Not because the board had been called but rather because after all those months of picking up, dropping off, paying for things, extending patience, and generally being kind to *Pansy*, they had turned on me in the worst of ways. They actually tried to get me fired for having a confrontation and grading appropriately. Neither she nor her mother had ever had a complaint about me until that day. It's one thing to get angry with someone; it's another to try to get them fired.

In the end, I was not fired although I did get a gentle but stern talking to by my principal about how when you're doing work that changes lives you have to be careful and how I needed to exercise more control over my temper. Her biggest concern however was my spirit because she could see that the incident left a serious dent. This was one of those rare moments, when an administrator looks at one of their passionate teachers, and just relates one teacher spirit to another. I thanked her and told her that I was fine, but I wasn't. I knew that I wasn't and that incident affected me for a long time. It still affects me now.

Pansy taught me about the unpredictable nature of the human spirit. Never in my wildest dreams would I have imagined that our relationship would have ended that way. We had never even had an argument up until that day. In retrospect, I wish that we had. Maybe we would have worked through more of the issues that existed beneath the dermis, that thick, sensitive layer of skin that contains nerve endings. In hindsight, I can think of many things that I should have done differently—one of them being to admit to myself how sick and tired I was of toting her around and not really seeing much growth. I should have contacted her parent to discuss some of my observations before things went sour. I never made her mom a partner in the mentoring of her daughter; I was satisfied that she allowed her to be involved. I should have kept a good anecdotal. I knew something was wrong with *Pansy,* and I knew that it centered around her emotions, but instead of working to get support for her, I attempted to mentor her through gentle nudging and cultural exposure and activities. A young woman that withdrawn and that would seek that level of vengeance clearly needed something more. I knew it. I think that I just didn't want to work that hard.

It may sound odd, but in a weird way, I thank *Pansy* for the experience. I treat emotional disorders far more seriously than I did when I first started Purple Rain. I even have a partner that introduced me to a counselor who is willing to counsel PR girls pro bono.

Mentors have to admit when something may be over their heads. If they decide to attempt to handle it alone, they must seek additional support in the best interest of the mentee. Support will help to protect the mentor as well. Effective mentoring cannot happen in a vacuum, but when it does, there is a price to pay and all parties involved end up losing.

Sometimes, there is no way to be completely sure if germination, which is the beginning growth of a seed or spore into a new individual, has taken place. If the seed has not taken deep enough roots, when the rough storms come, it will be washed away. This is what I experienced with *Loosestrife*. From the very beginning, *Loosestrife* was an exciting person to know. She was smart and energetic. She was one of the few kids genuinely interested in academics and extracurricular activities. She brought the full package. She could read, write, and she was a great speaker. I felt delighted that she was interested in Purple Rain. Of all the young women I inducted that evening, *Loosestrife* gave me the most pride. I saw myself in *Loosestrife*. I loved her outgoing and independent spirit, which was why it was difficult initially to see her fade away.

There was no one major incident that ever occurred between *Loosestrife* and me. There was, however, an accumulation of minor incidents that caused our relationship to wither. The first centered on a discrepancy about Avon orders. We sold Avon as a fundraiser. *Loosestrife* would turn in big orders, and at first her people paid for their orders in a timely matter—later, they did not . The way that Avon works is if you don't pay for the last order, you can't put in your new order and thus other people don't get their products. At first, in good faith, I'd pay for the orders, but then I had to start returning items and that meant that not only were we wasting time, and not making a profit, but we were also losing money.

The second incident centered on our book club. During book club, we had agreed that what was "spoken in book club would stay in book club." We had one girl that was in an abusive relationship, and her abuser attended the high school. The young woman was very open about the type of abuse that was happening to her on a day-to-day basis.

Loosestrife decided one day to say something to the boy about the abuse he inflicted on his girlfriend, which in turn brought further abuse on the young woman. After that, the girls didn't trust her, and they were careful of what they shared in front of her.

The third incident centered around how she treated one of the members of "Just Us Fellas" who expressed affection towards her. Just Us Fellas is our brother organization, and we collaborate with them over domestic violence issues. Because it is a male mentoring group, the young men exhibit very respectful behavior towards girls, and they are particularly supportive of PR girls. *Loosestrife* was essentially dishonest instead of telling the young man that she wasn't interested. She ignored him, ducked him, and distanced herself from him, which created a weird tension when we were all together. We later learned that she had affection for someone else, and she was keeping it a secret from all of us, which we never understood.

The final incident centered on *Pansy*. *Loosestrife* and *Pansy* were good friends and even though *Loosestrife* knew that Pansy had lied about everything from her schoolwork to the abortion, she remained committed to that friendship. In fact, she and *Pansy* would go into another teacher's room to eat lunch almost every day. Her choice to do that caused a huge rift in the group. A couple of girls expressed wanting to fight her because they questioned her loyalty. They couldn't understand why she would "kick it" with a cut throat and a liar. I had to remind them that violence wasn't what we were about. I did not like it, but I also understood that it was a high school and that *Loosestrife* had the right to be friends with anyone she chose, but her choice did make me pull back from her. *Pansy* and her mom had tried to destroy me. That wasn't something that I was able to overlook.

An adult came to me and told me that they had overheard *Loosestrife* sharing things that we'd discussed within our group with *Pansy*. My wounds were still open, and that information was a major hindrance to my own personal healing process. I began to experience days where it was difficult for me to look *Loosestrife* in the face. A blind man could see that our interaction was dramatically different; however, I never asked her to leave. I've never asked anyone to leave. My pulling back coupled with her other social set was just the right mixture to cause the leaves of our interpersonal communication to shrivel. Just like that, we didn't speak much anymore. It didn't help that *Loosestrife* stood us up for two very important events and then became offended when we'd moved on without her.

The final straw for me was when both the principal and another teacher approached me and said that *Loosestrife* wanted me to call her. They said that *Loosestrife* had confided in them that she really needed to speak with me but that she felt alienated and didn't know how to talk with me. Here was a girl that had been to my home, eaten at my dinner table, spent countless hours at activities, events, and on the phone, telling someone outside the group what she felt incapable of saying to me. I was so irritated and angry that I just shook my head and put my feet in the sand. I said that if she wanted to talk to me she would call. The onus wasn't on me; it was on her.

Loosestrife never called and neither did I. As far as I can tell, there were no hard feelings. She never went around bashing the group and we never bashed her. We had so much fun and exciting stuff going on truthfully, we didn't have time to. There were times that I honestly missed *Loosestrife*—her energy and enthusiasm. The way that she was open to more than just "Westside" hood thinking. She had been exposed to more

because she had grown up in Evanston, IL and spent the majority of her academic school life in that system, and that had made a world of difference in how she saw the world and herself in it.

After she left, I felt relieved on one hand and stuck on the other. When you are servicing some of the most left behind kids, it is hard to find kids not completely jaded, trapped in a cycle of cynical thoughts and overt put-downs. She was different because she was also a ward of the state, but unlike so many others, she was fun to know. She was not interested in wearing that fact as some badge of honor; if truth be told, she was silent about it for a long time. In spite of her modesty, I came to perceive her as the champion with the deceptive spirit.

Mentors have to accept that even when a mentee carries qualities that mirror their own, they are not that mentee. I minimized much of *Loosestrife's* behavior because I saw her as someone who just needed a little fine-tuning, much as I did when I was her age, and then she would be ready for the world. Later, I was forced to face the reality that although we were similar in personality and temperament, one distinguishing factor was that she was a ward of the state. That fact had not only made us different, it had also left her scathed. In the end, she was unable to filter elemental mediocrity. What she could not filter, she attached to it.

Falling Foliage

We were down to a solid four. The four that remained had survived witnessing seven of their inducted sister's fall away one after another within the first five months of memberships. I am sure that the things sustaining us at that time were our activities, workshops, and our partnerships. There is a piece of me that would like to believe that they grew to love one another and respect the work that I was putting into them as a mentor. I wanted to believe that we were an extended family, each finding a place, and individual space in which to grow. I thought the pruning of flowers was complete. Like the weatherman, I reported, "No signs of rain. Expect clear skies." In addition, like weathermen sometimes do, I came back to report that there was "an unexpected low pressure storm heading in from the Northern Hemisphere." It had a name: *Violet*.

I had known *Violet* prior to her ever-joining Purple Rain. I had her as a Spanish student. Besides being cute, *Violet* revealed no extra special qualities. She was not a natural leader, speaker, or writer; nonetheless, she enjoyed being a part of Purple Rain. She brought a rather positive energy. She was easy to talk to, and she behaved appropriately out in public. Other than the fact that I didn't agree with the level of support that she offered her friend, who was in an abusive relationship, I really didn't have very many complaints about her. I thought that she should step up more, but I figured that we had time to work on that. Besides, learning to support victims of domestic violence was addressed as part of our book club and our regular meetings. Her thinking seemed to be getting better. I concluded that with regular watering and sunshine, she would bloom into a beautiful flower.

As part of an ongoing fundraiser, our club sold water. In general, if I was busy I trusted the girls to go into our classroom refrigerator and get it. I also trusted them with money. I spent the money that we raised from any fundraiser that we had on them. They were well aware of that fact because they were rarely required to pay for anything, which included food, transportation, t-shirts, and admission. I worked hard to offset the cost of things so that wouldn't be an excuse for them not to attend events.

Violet stayed at about 95% attendance, which meant she directly benefited from the money raised. This is why I was stunned and amazed when after asking me to get a bottle of water for another girl to purchase; she attempted to steal one for herself. I caught her and confronted her, and she admitted the attempted theft. I asked her why she hadn't just asked me for one, and she couldn't explain why. I had never known *Violet* to steal directly; I had however experienced her borrowing money and not paying it back. She was the princess of that behavior. She was also not a giver. I remember one of my mentee's giving me a Hello Kitty bracelet for my birthday, and as she was handing it to me, *Violet* quickly shouted that the gift was from both of them. There was even an occasion when she brought me some balloons for my birthday that I later learned had been taken from in front of a display that sat outside of a business. As deceitful as that may sound, I saw it as a character flaw that was being addressed without totally putting her on the spot.

In retrospect, I know that I was practicing miss-targeted mentoring. *Violet* functioned in the middle ground, drawing no special attention and creating no special stir; however, her occasional deceitful behavior was a cry for help. Along with all the other things that I addressed, I needed to give her lessons on ethics. Petty thieves steal all the time. They tend to view one's trust and openness as an opportunity. I don't think for one minute that *Violet's* stealing of a water bottle was personal to me. I think that she called herself "getting over" and that wherever she went, she carried that mindset. The fact that I trusted her made me a "sucker" in her mind. The code on the street is that you take advantage of a sucker whether you have to or not.

Although *Violet* paid me back—in fact, I made her pay back all the money that she owed me—I still couldn't help but distance myself from her. I couldn't trust her, and that knowledge changed the entire dynamics of our relationship. She no longer felt comfortable being around me. The beautiful easiness that had once flowed between had been destroyed with the stealing of a $1.00 bottle of water. I told the group that *Violet* was welcome to attend any meeting or event; however, there would no longer be any exchange of money, and I did not intend to sponsor her admission to events. That bottle had bought her financial independence from Purple Rain. I wanted her to think about it every time she reached in her pockets to pay for something that she had stolen from her own group.

Like the leaf that begins to wither because it has lost its connection to its direct source of water, *Violet* dropped off and blew away. On occasion, I get an email or she will post a tag on our web journal expressing that she misses us. I am always happy to see that she still thinks about the group. Sometimes I dream that she has become a self-reflective young woman, strong enough to call and apologize, willing to explain what was wrong with that behavior. I would love to see that kind of growth from her. It has not happened as of yet, but there is still the possibility.

Mentors have to be sure to teach a code of ethics as part of their program. Some may think that teaching ethics is obsolete, but I have found that just like the breaking down of the nuclear family, lack of ethics has left society with a litany of problems to solve. It is difficult to navigate in this world without a system of moral standards. Never has it been more important to teach our youth the appropriate conduct for an individual or group than today. Violet *stands as both an example and a casualty* of that fact.

Then there were three. *Petunia* was invested, caring, and enthusiastic about anything Purple Rain. She was our greatest cheerleader. Every place she went, she sang our praises. PR had given her a place to belong. It had made it possible for her to make friends. Prior to joining, high school was difficult for *Petunia* because she was teased. Someone was always talking about her glasses and her appearance; however, in the club she flourished. I pushed her to talk. Before long, she was writing, speaking, and performing. Within a short time, *Petunia* had earned the respect of much of the school body. Than there was *Wisteria,* She was committed, bubbly, and concerned. I could always count on *Wisteria* to be present at any event that we were having. In fact, she would be one of the first to arrive. She had originally approached me about when PR would begin meeting. It was clear that she was very excited. She expressed great affection for me as well. She even went as far as to label me her "godmother," something that I allowed but never fully embraced. I believed that a "godmother" was a woman who sponsored a child at baptism and that she is viewed as being equivalent to the maternal parent. In the case of death, she agrees to assume responsibility for the child's religious upbringing. *Wisteria* and I hadn't known one another but a couple of months; furthermore, I had no real relationship with her parent other than her occasional attendance at events. Our relationship was further complicated by the fact that when we were left one on one, we really had nothing to say to one another. The only thing that we genuinely shared in common was our love for dancing. I was never quite sure why she was in Purple Rain because she never enjoyed writing or speaking, even though she would do it for the group. I was left to assume, because of her regular attendance and her mother's insistence that she stay involved, that she had

to be getting something out of it. Finally, there was *Wildflower*—confused, abused, and full of love. She was the only member that was actively in an abusive relationship.

It is always interesting in the mentoring process how some mentee's stand out from the rest. You always have at least one mentee that just completely captures your heart—and it's usually not someone that you would expect. That is how *Wildflower* was for me. I knew *Wildflower* from another girls group, and although the spirit behind putting that group together was positive, I became discouraged with it. We were doing a lot of talking about nothing. I never felt like we were really getting to the real issues, the self-hate issues, those things that destroy your character and turn you into a professional thoughtless follower. I really didn't have a lot of control over the things that we discussed because the woman that put it together really didn't want to collaborate. Of course, when she initially approached me, she claimed that she did but in reality, it was "her way or the highway." I fought with myself a long time about it, but I chose the highway, which meant that I didn't get to know *Wildflower* very well.

I am a strong believer that all things happen for a reason and usually in due time you will learn why. A couple of years later, I would start my own girls group, Purple Rain. Although I had seen *Wildflower* around over the years, this time she was my student and one of the very first girls to express genuine interest in checking out PR.

I didn't know at the time that she was in an abusive relationship. She seemed like such a happy, bubbly spirit that I thought she was checking out PR because she enjoyed my class and she remembered me from the previous group. As PR grew and the activities and the curriculum pressed forward, so did her willingness to open and share. Eventually, she felt strong enough to completely open her "Pandora's Box," which meant two things: one, the real work began and two, the authentic person showed up. I thought that I liked her before when she was hiding behind fake smiles; I really liked her once she was able to shed some layers of pain through laughter and tears and soul searching.

I don't want to leave anyone with the wrong impression. *Wildflower* did many of the annoying things that all the other mentee's did; for example, she claimed that she would attend an event and then not show up. Occasionally when asked to speak, she would play down her smarts. When directed towards a positive outlet or an opportunity that would take her skill level further, she would decide without speaking with me not to do it—the list could really go on. What made *Wildflower* special and different from everyone else was that *Wildflower* liked love. She would rather be nice than any other thing. She never did anything with ill intentions. Usually, if she let you down, she would beat herself up more than you could imagine. She was also the only mentee who would tell me the complete truth. If *Wildflower* were going to tell it, she would tell it all. She would not sit and feed you half the story. She would allow herself to be vulnerable enough to share the complete story even if she looked unflattering in it. She was the only mentee that would immediately say that she was sorry and attempt to adjust her behavior.

The things described may not seem like much, or maybe you think that these are things that she should have been doing anyway; however, to get the full scope of what made *Wildflower* stand out, you have to understand that not only was *Wildflower* dating an abuser but also all of her friends and her immediate family interacted with him. She received messages all day long that the person that choked, bit, slapped, and hit her wasn't that bad after all. He couldn't be that bad or others wouldn't continue to socialize with him. Enablers surrounded her, and every time she showed up to an event, it was a miracle.

The very people that should have been protecting her, helped keep her stuck in that relationship. The only pure voices of reason came from Purple Rain or our brother organization, Just Us Fellas. Everyone else told *Wildflower* that she was stupid or they would tell her to leave him, but they would continue to invite him to social events. Some of them even went as far as to report information about her actions or whereabouts to him. Purple Rain and Just Us Fellas members were the only people with whom she could feel safe and happy.

Once I discovered that, I kept *Wildflower* with me as much as possible and I bestowed her with many responsibilities. With each assignment and success, *Wildflower* began to see more clearly; she started actually questioning her friendships, and more importantly, she began to question her relationship with him.

Wildflower literally fought to grow and change. Unlike the other girls, she knew what was coming when she didn't call when she said that she would or when she attended an event that he didn't want her to attend. She was the only "Raindrop" getting regularly beat up, yet she tried to attend everything. One of the best things that happened was that her cell phone broke. He could no longer track her every move and had lost one of his favorite tools for cursing her out. He would make her feel bad in the middle of book club or before an event. It was so frustrating for the other "Raindrops" to watch her still call him or go see him and then learn just how mean he had been to her—and believe me, he was mean.

The entire group was angry after learning that he had pinned her down and bitten her face. She treated it very nonchalantly, but we knew it hurt her, and to be honest it hurt us. We were furious. Some of the girls wanted to report him to the police, but they learned in book club that the fight had to come out of the victim. If she wasn't ready to confront him and take things to a legal level, it was a waste of time. She would only return to him.

Her choices kept me sad and often angry with him, with her, with her family, and with the abuse, but *Wildflower* made me grow. She single handedly caused me to grow more and work harder for and in Purple Rain than any other member. She made me remember past pain when I was "sucker punched" and my glasses were broken on my face. She also made me remember past love when I was naïve enough to believe that I could love my abuser out of tantrums and bouts of rage even if it meant sacrificing my whole self.

I shared things with *Wildflower* that I never shared with any of the other "Raindrops" simply because she needed me to. I have written things to her and about her. I even performed a piece that I wrote for her in hopes of reaching her. I was always looking for ways to help her relate various issues that have arisen out of our girl chat. Through all the craziness, I had to accept that she was a woman-becoming, needing guidance to get through the process. Whoever said becoming a woman was easy lied. I discovered that every time I helped *Wildflower*. Like so many young women with a predisposition to love hard, becoming a woman was overwhelming. Trying to develop while being beaten made her coming of age close to impossible. She was meant to be in my life and I in hers. It became an honor to share in the mentoring experience with such a beautiful bruised flower. Besides, every time I held her hand, I healed a piece of myself.

Recently, I purchased a shirt for Black History Month that has a quote on it by Harriet Tubman. It says, "I freed hundreds of slaves, could've freed thousands if they only knew themselves." When I saw that shirt, I had to have it. I just couldn't leave the store without purchasing it. I related to it so strongly. It just seemed to capture this intense essence of truth, which is that the key to freedom of any kind is knowing your self, recognizing your value. Nothing replaces self-realization and self-worth. I have been fighting everyday to get *Wildflower* as well as my other mentees to know "themselves." With some of them, it has been a losing battle, but every now and then I win, which means that there is one more flower to add to the world's bouquet.

Mentors have to embrace the definition of what it means to be a mentor, which is somebody, usually older and more experienced, who provides advice and support to, and watches over and fosters the progress of, a younger, less experienced person. Mentoring often requires us to walk beside our mentee, many times holding their hands when strong winds bring on insecurity; however, it also requires us to know when to let their hands loose and continue to guide them with our hearts. If we teach well enough, our mentees will act as mentors to someone else someday.

She Lets Him In

She lets him in
Every time
She lets him in
Her mind
Her heart
Her head
And Always
Her bed
When he's not
With others
However,
The issue
Isn't really
Additional lovers
They form their
Own quilt of shame
The issue is
Her speechless daze
And how she sits
Seemingly unfazed
When she explains
How,
In a clever act of wickedness
He leaned in
As if to kiss
Her
And instead
Bit her
Face

It bled a little and
Like a grain of grit
Little is how she felt
Little is what is left
Of the circular mark
With tiny ridges
That darkened and

Sat misplaced
On her caramel skin
She still lets him in
Though the moon refuses
To lend light to their nights and
The sun's visor partially
Blocks their day's rays
She stays
And prays
As she lays on pillows
Stuffed with purplish blue secrets
That seeps through tiny ring shaped holes
Exposing multiple layers of humiliation
Birth from simple situations
He argues about everything
Old and new

She says, what can I do?
It don't make a difference
About my existence
I can't handle his persistence
To control
My mind
My heart
My head
And definitely
My bed
I know he has supplemental flames
He makes it plain
For all to see
He boldly
Disrespects me
When I try to fight
Or attempt to defy his wishes
He hits me with a litany of

Bitches
Bust downs
And Hoes

And like porcelain
Struck by a sledge hammer
I shatter.
So it don't matter
Besides, I love him

Like a professional athlete
She practices her grin
 As if a heart, wrapped in cataract
She beats for more within
Though he extends oil slicked hands
She passes him her heart
Any glimmer of kindness
She takes as a start
A chance
A sign that his abuse
Is only in her mind
It's only for a moment
He really loves her
He just don't know it

As if stuck on a faulty ferris wheel
She don't know
How to get down
And heal the circular mark
With the tiny ridges
That remains dark and misplaced
On her now blemished skin
Instead Twenty-four-seven
Three-six-five
She stays in constant rotation
And like the pin wheel

That depends on wind
She continues to let him in
And perpetually spin.
Unable to clock out
Trained to give in
She blows her feelings
Into balloons and
With bowed head
She watches helplessly
As he slowly
Releases them every day
She says, "It don't matter anyway
Besides, I love him"

A storm is an atmospheric disturbance manifested in strong winds accompanied by rain, snow, hail, or sleet and often by thunder and lightning. The storm center is a focus of trouble, disturbance, or controversy.

By the end of the school year, I was determined to celebrate the small successes, those things that are overlooked when one views them through the eye of the storm. In spite of the unraveling that occurred after the Induction Ceremony, the storm had not washed away all my seeds of optimism. Purple Rain had so much to celebrate. Our girls participated in the Clothesline Project, the Vagina Monologues, and a documentary produced by Columbia College students on domestic violence. They wrote, filmed, directed, and edited their own music video. They had two articles written about their group in two separate newspapers. They participated in workshops centered on HIV & AIDS, Hip-Hop Culture, and Anti-Hate. They were guest speakers at the fifth Annual Chicago land Youth Against Aids Conference, and the Coalition on Adolescent Risk Reduction. They were even included in a promotional film for School Street Movement. Our girls attended far too many spoken word sets to mention and best of all they spent the entire year writing. They were a part of an all women's writing circle, which was not only therapeutic but also empowering. It gave them the material that they used to perform with; it also gave them the material that they needed to start healing.

Other girls at AASTA High School had an opportunity to experience Purple Rain programming through our poet's hour, steppers sets, and service learning projects. Our service learning did everything from collecting teddy bears for the littlest victims of domestic violence to collecting and delivering toiletries to an all women's shelter. We raised money for both Haiti and Tsunami relief efforts. I don't think anyone could forget the powerful Women's History Month workshops and activities. As a club, we had managed to mentor the whole woman, and if no one else grew from that feat, I did.

My mentoring journey had taken me places that I had intended and it had exposed attitudes that I could never have predicted. I was unprepared for the depth of indifference that existed among the staff and permeated our school. It was astonishing to see how some of the staff ignored, blocked, complained, and in some cases, bluntly put down the work that Purple Rain was doing. Unlike an athletic department, Purple Rain was not respected as being part of the backbone of the school even though one of its veteran teachers led it and it dealt with many of the social and emotional problems of our students. I contribute most of that attitude to the principal's sluggish support. Although she allowed PR to flow freely there, she reluctantly gave it her anointing, which set up this weird dichotomy of them vs. us. The school saw PR as "Ms. Evans's group" instead of AASTA's own. There was little to no acknowledgement of the successes of our youth. The adult staff attended roughly 10% of the events that our youth were involved in, and it did not matter whether it was in or out of the school. It wouldn't have been as bad if the staff had regularly congratulated them, but most times the kids came back to silence, a cold climate of insensitivity which inflicted a quiet pain in all of our spirits.

What that staff failed to understand is that we teach our students by the words we speak and our actions, and when our actions are negative, they drown out our words completely. The staff claimed to want to see positive behavior from the student body, but their disinterest taught the youth to say to me, "These teachers only have something to say when you're doing something wrong." I had to agree with them, and then I had to fight vigorously the negative blows to their sense of self-worth that attempted to seep within.

There is a piece of me that understands the apathy that exists at our school. It has been coined a "Failing school," and in the ten years that I have been there it has seen five principals. "No Child Left Behind" laws caused massive teacher and paraprofessional turnover, which resulted in the loss of many of the great professionals that invested in both the students and their community. It has been Reconstituted, Intervened, and converted to small schools all the while attempting to raise the test scores of the most left behind kids in the city. The teachers work under intense scrutiny. There are always many meetings, new programs, little planning time, and less subject specific collaboration. In general, good teachers there work hard and get very little praise. Terrible teachers can hide behind red tape and poor micro management, which builds resentment. Inadvertently, many teachers have transferred their frustration and demoralization onto the kids.

The school climate made mentoring harder than it had to be. The mentees and their issues were one thing, but the battles that had to be wedged amongst the adult staff left me feeling tormented. It was a vivid example of exactly why Purple Rain needed to exist in the school. There were moments that I allowed myself to be captured in the winds of hate while other times, I sat alone, frustrated and depressed. I felt as though I was just spinning wheels. I couldn't understand why certain teachers would function as saboteurs at a school full of DCFS children, grandma babies, pregnant teens, and second- and third-year freshmen. Why hadn't many of them recognized that traditional teaching was not working? Having worked there a while,

I knew that this was the last stop for many of the youth. I have the obituaries to prove it. I knew that if we did not reach them now, they would be lost in a cycle of oppression. The thought was so depressing.

Mentors are very susceptible to depression because they are often leading with their hearts. I fought and prayed for my release; however, I was left too tired to look for the "one red rose among the weeds." Like the girls I serviced, I was instead looking for relief, a place to rest my war torn spirit, an answer to all my confusion. I was sick of all of it, and I do mean sick. I had packed on twenty pounds, I was suffering from chronic insomnia, and for the first time in my life, my blood pressure was high. I wanted to shut down Purple Rain. I spent many nights scolding myself for even starting the group. I questioned what I had gotten myself into; I concluded that I would never invest in youth again, once I got myself out.

In the book, *Prayers of a Dedicated Teacher*, a section reads, "As citizens of a fast-changing world, we face challenges that sometimes leave us feeling overworked, overcommitted, and overwhelmed. However, God has different plans for us. He intends that we slow down long enough to praise Him and to glorify His Son. When we do, He lifts our spirits and enriches our lives."

It was time for me to scale down and nothing spoke louder to me on that point than my blood pressure. I began to prepare for a sabbatical to California. I was offered all kinds of overtime and summer school money; I turned it all down. It was time to let loose of the guilt that often accompanies mentoring, which causes mentors to feel bad when they focus on their own personal needs. My health was screaming to me to scale back. I listened and I cut PR's pace by two thirds. I finished out my prior commitments, but I refused to add anything additional. I decreased contact with the girls. If they called me, I was there for them, but I did virtually no soliciting. I started focusing on assisting Just Us Fellas on a limited scale because they were experiencing a string of successes with their spoken word and their workshops. My being around their positive energy functioned as a fog clearer. It reminded me of how exciting it is to see young people shed negative layers and step into greatness. I was feeling better, but I still resolved to formally announce the end of Purple Rain. I could not imagine a repeat of our first year of existence.

Life is full of surprises and as cliché as it may be it is true. Just when I thought I had had enough, God sent me two tiny glimmers of hope by the names of *Ever Blooming* and *Angel fire*. Their enthusiastic faces reminded me of my calling, my mission to shape and help mold the minds and lives of our youth. I could not turn them away. I was going to take my sabbatical; however, Purple Rain was not going anywhere. In fact, it was just beginning anew. *Ever blooming and Angel fire* were assurances of that fact.

After the storm, I was weather worn, tired, and tattered. What began as sympathy grew into a "cause." It was more than lunchroom conversation or a new spoken word piece. It had become a mission, which is nothing more than love with legs, running in an effort to change things.

In August 2005, Purple Rain officially turned 1 year old, and it is doing what one-year-olds do. It is growing, learning, falling down, and getting back up. It laughs and it cries. It celebrates successes and becomes angry over defeats, but it is still here. My sabbatical was life changing. I lost 30 pounds, lowered my blood pressure, confronted some fears, and I made some life long friends. I had

attempted the impossible; teaching full time and running a full fledge mentoring program while balancing my family commitment. A quote says, "Anyone can steer in calm waters…. But opportunities go to those who weather the storms." I had weathered the storm.

Purple Rain: Girls Overcoming Abuse *"changing the world one raindrop at a time."*

Mentoring is a commitment. It is not about "drop-in" programs or "take a kid to work" day. It not about preaching or showing off your expensive house as proof to them that with hard work, they can have one, too. It is about investment, a pledge of the heart, to give when you think that you cannot give anymore, to find space to pump love when their pulse feels low, to hold another up when there is potential for growth. Like it or not, mentors have to be willing to grow, too. They must not expect that their growth will be an easy process; like the youth they mentor, it will be painstaking, and full of trial and error, but it is necessary and valuable for all parties involved. I said earlier that this book is about all the purple petals and bruised flowers that I have nurtured on my road to enlightenment and self-love. I learned to include myself. I was "called" to be a mentor. I accept.

Printed in the United States
By Bookmasters